Good Friends Are Like Angels
They Add Blessings to Life

Artwork by **Claire Stoner**

HARVEST HOUSE PUBLISHERS

EUGENE, OREGON

Good Friends Are Like Angels

Artwork Copyright © 2010 by Claire Stoner

Published by Harvest House Publishers
Eugene, Oregon 97402
www.harvesthousepublishers.com

ISBN 978-0-7369-2582-2

Artwork designs are reproduced under license © 2010 by Claire Stoner and may not be reproduced without permission. For more information regarding the use of this artwork, contact:

Clair Stoner LLC
Two Jefferson Court
New Freedom, Pennsylvania 17349
www.ClairesStudioLLC.com

Design and production by Garborg Design Works, Savage, Minnesota

Harvest House Publishers has made every effort to trace the ownership of all poems and quotes. In the event of a question arising from the use of a poem or quote, we regret any error made and will be pleased to make the necessary correction in future editions of this book.

Verses are taken from the New American Standard Bible ®, © 1960, 1962, 1963, 1968, 1971, 1972, 1973, 1975, 1977, 1995 by The Lockman Foundation. Used by permission. (www.Lockman.org); from The Message. Copyright © by Eugene H. Peterson 1993, 1994, 1995, 1996, 2000, 2001, 2002. Used by permission of NavPress Publishing Group; and from the Revised Standard Version of the Bible, copyright © 1946, 1952, 1971 by the Division of Christian Education of the National Council of the Churches of Christ in the U.S.A. Used by permission. All rights reserved.

Printed in China

16 / FC / 10 9

Friendship is
a strong
and habitual
inclination in
two persons
to promote
the good
and happiness
of one another.

EUSTACE BUDGELL

For friendship, of itself a holy tie,
is made more sacred by adversity.

JOHN DRYDEN

Peace is the first thing the

Friendship is the only cement that will ever hold the world together.

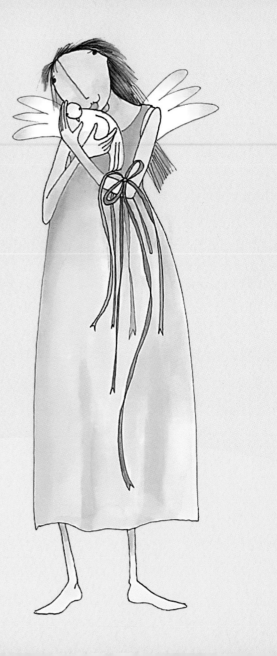

angels sang.

5

A friend is a present you give yourself.

ROBERT LOUIS STEVENSON

If we would build on a sure foundation in friendship, we must love friends for their sake rather than for our own.

CHARLOTTE BRONTË

I keep my friends as misers do their treasure, because, of all the things granted us by wisdom, none is greater or better than friendship.

PIETRO ARETINO

Every blade of grass has an angel bending over it saying, "Grow, grow."

JEWISH PROVERB

To the world you may be just one person, but to one person you may be the world.

BRANDI SNYDER

Life has no blessing like a prudent friend.

EURIPIDES

Love is a song the heart sings.

Friendship that flows from the heart cannot be frozen by adversity, as the water that flows from the spring cannot congeal in winter.

JAMES FENIMORE COOPER

Good friends are good for your health.

SYDNEY SMITH

Friendships are fragile things and require as much care

Angels encourage
everyone in the
right direction...up.

AUTHOR UNKNOWN

in handling as any other fragile and precious thing. RANDOLPH S. BOURNE

One friend in a
lifetime is much,
two are many,
three are hardly
possible. Friendship
needs a certain
parallelism of life,
a community
of thought,
a rivalry of aim.

HENRY BROOKS ADAMS

Angels promote closeness and foster tenderness.

AUTHOR UNKNOWN

Silently one by one,
In the infinite meadows of heaven,
Blossomed the lovely stars,
The forget-me-nots of the angels.

HENRY WADSWORTH LONGFELLOW

Friendship is genuine when two friends can enjoy each other's company without speaking a word to one another.

GEORGE EBERS

A friend is, as it were, a second self.

MARCUS T. CICERO

17

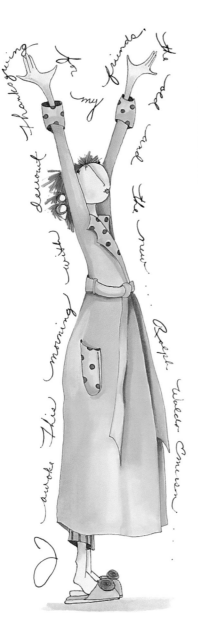

Hush, my dear, lie still and slumber,
Holy angels guard thy bed!
Heavenly blessings without number
Gently falling on thy head.

ISAAC WATTS

Friendship is the
shadow of the
evening, which
strengthens with the
setting sun of life.

JEAN DE LA FONTAINE

Friends do not live in harmony merely, as some say, but in melody.

HENRY DAVID THOREAU

Thy care has preserved my spirit.

Kindness in words creates
confidence. Kindness in
thinking creates profoundness.
Kindness in giving creates love.

LAO TZU

20

A friend is sensitive
to the person you
are. She listens
both to the words
you say and to the
ones you don't say.
She sees you,
and she loves what
she sees, and
somehow you like
yourself better when
you're together.

DONNA OTTO AND EMILIE BARNES

You are as welcome as flowers in May.

CHARLES MACKLIN

True friendship is a plant of slow growth,
and must undergo the shocks of adversity
before it is entitled to the appellation.

GEORGE WASHINGTON

We see them not—we cannot hear
The music of their wings—
Yet know we that they sojourn near,
The Angels of the spring!

They glide along this lovely ground
When the first violet grows;
Their graceful hands have just unbound
The zone of yonder rose.

ROBERT STEPHEN HAWKER

Few delights can equal the mere presence of one whom we utterly trust.

GEORGE MACDONALD

I am treating you as my friend asking you share my present minuses in the hope I can ask you to share my future pluses.

KATHERINE MANSFIELD

When it hurts to look back, and you're too scared to look ahead, just look beside you and your best friend will be there.

AUTHOR UNKNOWN

Thankful

am I.

A sweet
friendship
refreshes
the soul.

THE BOOK OF PROVERBS

To each one of us friendship has a different meaning. For all of us it is a gift. Friendship needs to be cherished and nurtured. It needs to be cultivated on a daily basis. Then shall it germinate and yield its fruit.

AUTHOR UNKNOWN

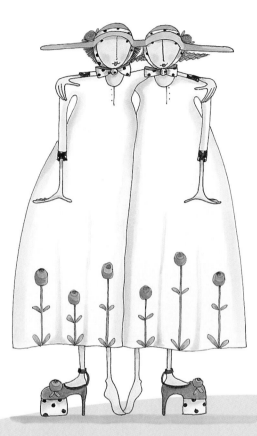

Friendship makes
prosperity brighter,
while it lightens
adversity by sharing
its griefs and anxieties.

MARCUS CICERO

Some friendships are as comforting and comfortable as a well-worn pair of
shoes. Others are full of excitement and adventure. The best ones are laced with
laughter and softened with tears and strengthened with a spiritual bond.

DONNA OTTO AND EMILIE BARNES

Agreement in likes and dislikes—this, and this only, is what constitutes true friendship.

CATILINE (LUCIUS SERGIUS CATILINA)

You are a letter

Spirit.

written

THE BOOK OF II CORINTHIANS

not with ink but with the

It is easy to say how we
love new friends, and
what we think of them,
but words can never
trace out all the fibers
that knit us to the old.

GEORGE ELIOT

I will not wish thee riches nor the glow
of greatness, but that wherever thou go
some weary heart shall gladden at thy smile,
or shadowed life know sunshine for awhile.
And so thy path shall be a track of light,
like angels' footsteps passing through the night.

WORDS ON A CHURCH WALL IN UPWALTHAM, ENGLAND

Friendship is a sheltering tree.

SAMUEL TAYLOR COLERIDGE

There are persons so radiant, so
genial, so kind, so pleasure-bearing,
that you instinctively feel in their
presence that they do you good,
whose coming into a room is like
the bringing of a lamp there.

HENRY WARD BEECHER

But friendship is
precious, not only
in the shade, but
in the sunshine
of life; and thanks
to a benevolent
arrangement of
things, the greater
part of life is sunshine.

THOMAS JEFFERSON

33

Blessed are they who have the gift of making

Ah, how good it feels!
The hand of an old friend.

HENRY WADSWORTH LONGFELLOW

Perhaps the most delightful
friendships are those in which
there is much agreement,
much disputation, and yet
more personal liking.

GEORGE ELIOT

friends, for it is one of God's greatest gifts.

THOMAS HUGHES

Trust is the sweet, solid foundation in your relationship with a friend. You trust her to hold close the private things you reveal to her. Your bedrock confidence is that she truly wants the best for you, whatever that best may be.

DONNA OTTO AND EMILIE BARNES

Let me benefit from you in the Lord; refresh my heart in Christ.

THE BOOK OF PHILEMON

The simplest things—
a gentle word,
a soothing touch—
bring joy and peace
like summer rain.

DINAH MARIA MULAK CRAIK

Then come the wild weather, come sleet or come snow,
We will stand by each other, however it blow.

SIMON DACH

She threw her arms around the Lion's neck and kissed him, patting his big head tenderly. Then she kissed the Tin Woodsman…she hugged the soft, stuffed body of the Scarecrow in her arms instead of kissing his painted face, and found she was crying herself at this sorrowful parting from her loving comrades.

Dorothy now took Toto up solemnly in her arms, and having said one last good-bye she clapped the heels of her shoes together three times, saying, "Take me home to Aunt Em!"

L. FRANK BAUM, *THE WIZARD OF OZ*

O continue thy steadfast love to those who know thee.

THE BOOK OF PSALMS

Do not forget to entertain

strangers, for by so doing

some people have entertained

angels without knowing it.

THE BOOK OF HEBREWS

40

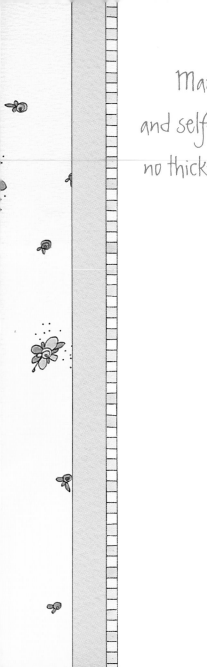

Many a friendship—long, loyal,
and self-sacrificing—rested at first upon
no thicker a foundation than a kind word.

FREDERICK W. FABER

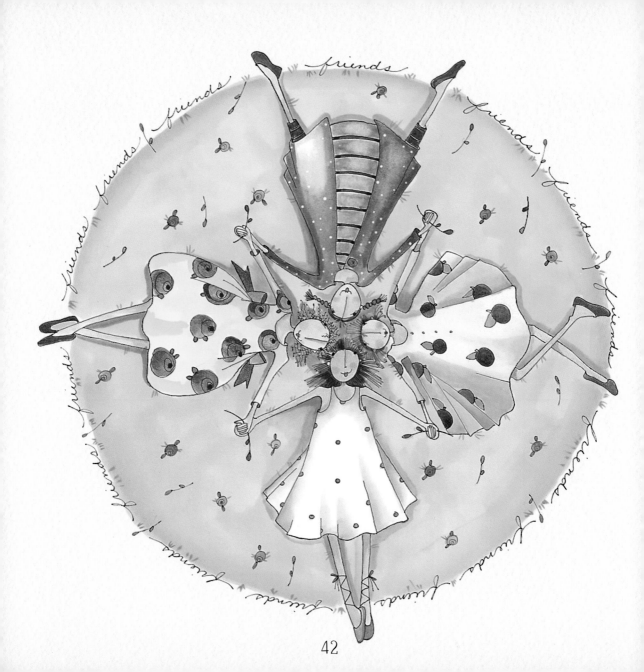

"Friends of the heart" are unforgettable people who, for whatever reason, stake a permanent claim there. These are our chosen sisters—the ones who leave us pondering what we did to deserve them. Best of all, they feel the same way about us.

DONNA OTTO AND EMILIE BARNES

When I find myself fading, I close my eyes and realize my friends are my energy.

AUTHOR UNKNOWN

43

An angel doesn't
have to be physical...
to touch you.

Friendship
is the pleasing
game of
interchanging
praise.

Friendship is a spiritual thing. It is
independent of matter or space
or time. That which I love in my
friend is not that which I see.
What influences me in my friend
is not his body, but his spirit.

Angels paint with sound
and sing with color.

AUTHOR UNKNOWN

So then we pursue the
things which make for
peace and the building
up of one another.

THE BOOK OF ROMANS

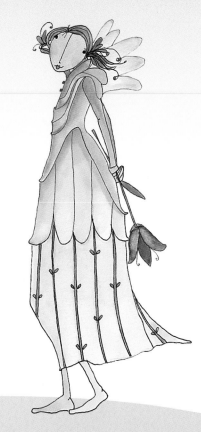

Great souls by instinct to each other turn,
Demand alliance, and in friendship burn.

JOSEPH ADDISON

47

A friend loves at all times.

THE BOOK OF PROVERBS

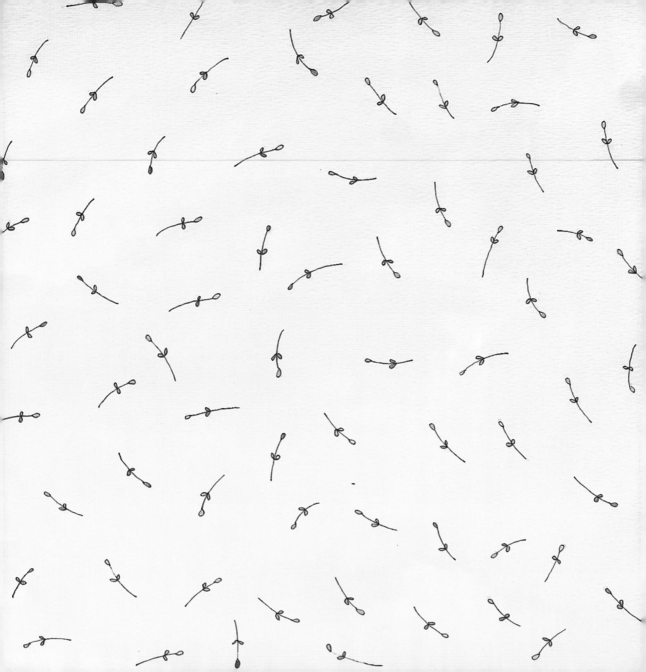